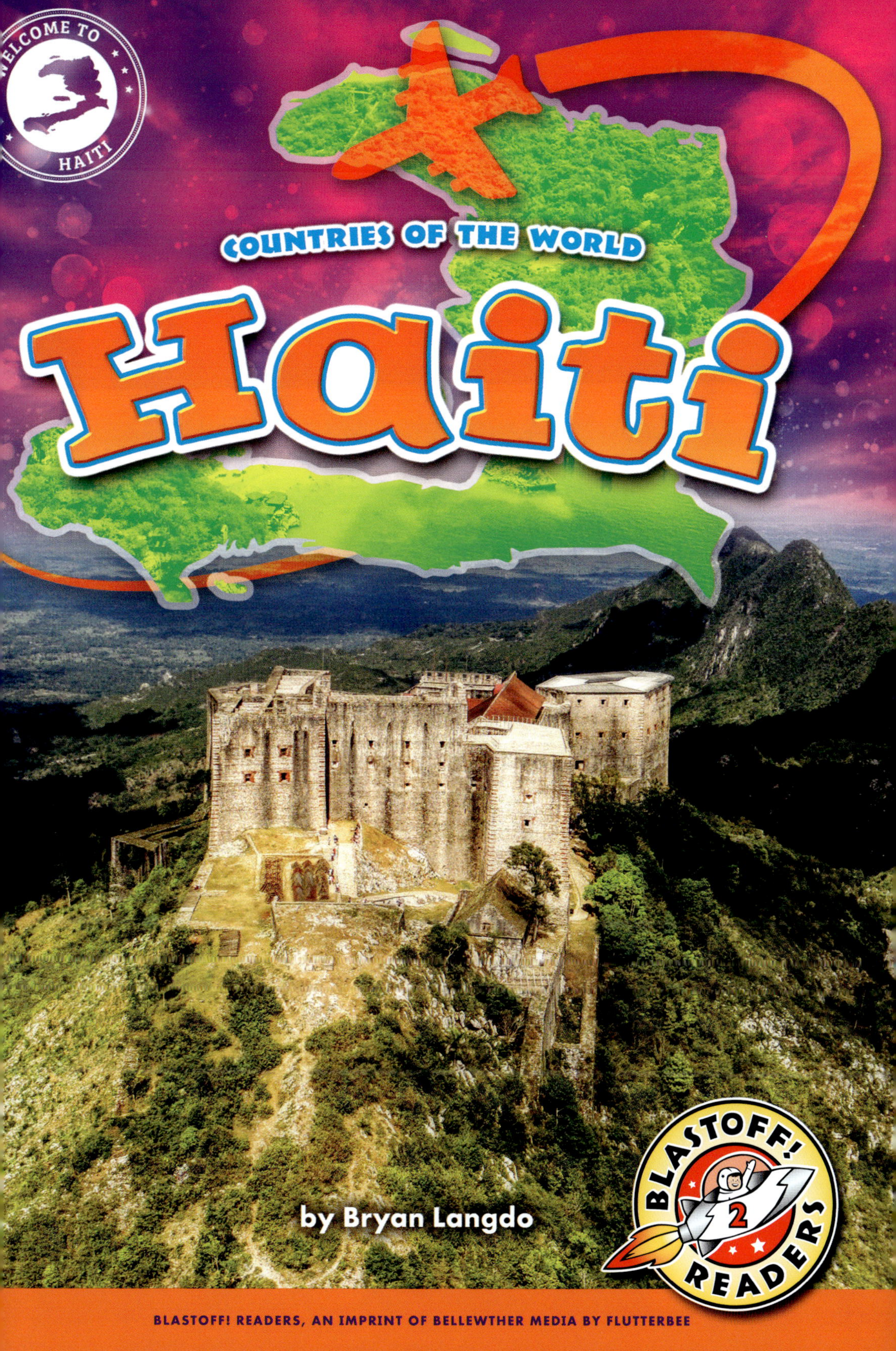
WELCOME TO
HAITI
COUNTRIES OF THE WORLD
Haiti
by Bryan Langdo
BLASTOFF!
2
READERS
BLASTOFF! READERS, AN IMPRINT OF BELLWETHER MEDIA BY FLUTTERBEE

**Blastoff! Readers** are carefully developed by literacy experts to build reading stamina and move students toward fluency by combining standards-based content with developmentally appropriate text.

**Level 1** provides the most support through repetition of high-frequency words, light text, predictable sentence patterns, and strong visual support.

**Level 2** offers early readers a bit more challenge through varied sentences, increased text load, and text-supportive special features.

**Level 3** advances early-fluent readers toward fluency through increased text load, less reliance on photos, advancing concepts, longer sentences, and more complex special features.

★ **Blastoff! Universe**

Reading Level

Blastoff! Beginners — Grade K

Grades 1–3

Grade 4

This edition first published in 2026 by Bellwether Media, Inc.



For information regarding permission, write to Bellwether Media, Inc., Attention: Permissions Department, 3500 American Blvd W, Suite 150, Bloomington, MN 55431.

Library of Congress Cataloging-in-Publication Data is available at www.loc.gov or upon request from the publisher.

ISBN: 9798893047837 (hardcover)
ISBN: 9798893048834 (paperback)

Editor: Rachael Barnes Designer: Brittany McIntosh

Printed in the United States of America, North Mankato, MN.

# Table of Contents

# All About Haiti

Haiti is a small country in the Caribbean Sea. Its capital is Port-au-Prince.

Haiti is part of **Hispaniola**. The Dominican Republic lies in the east.

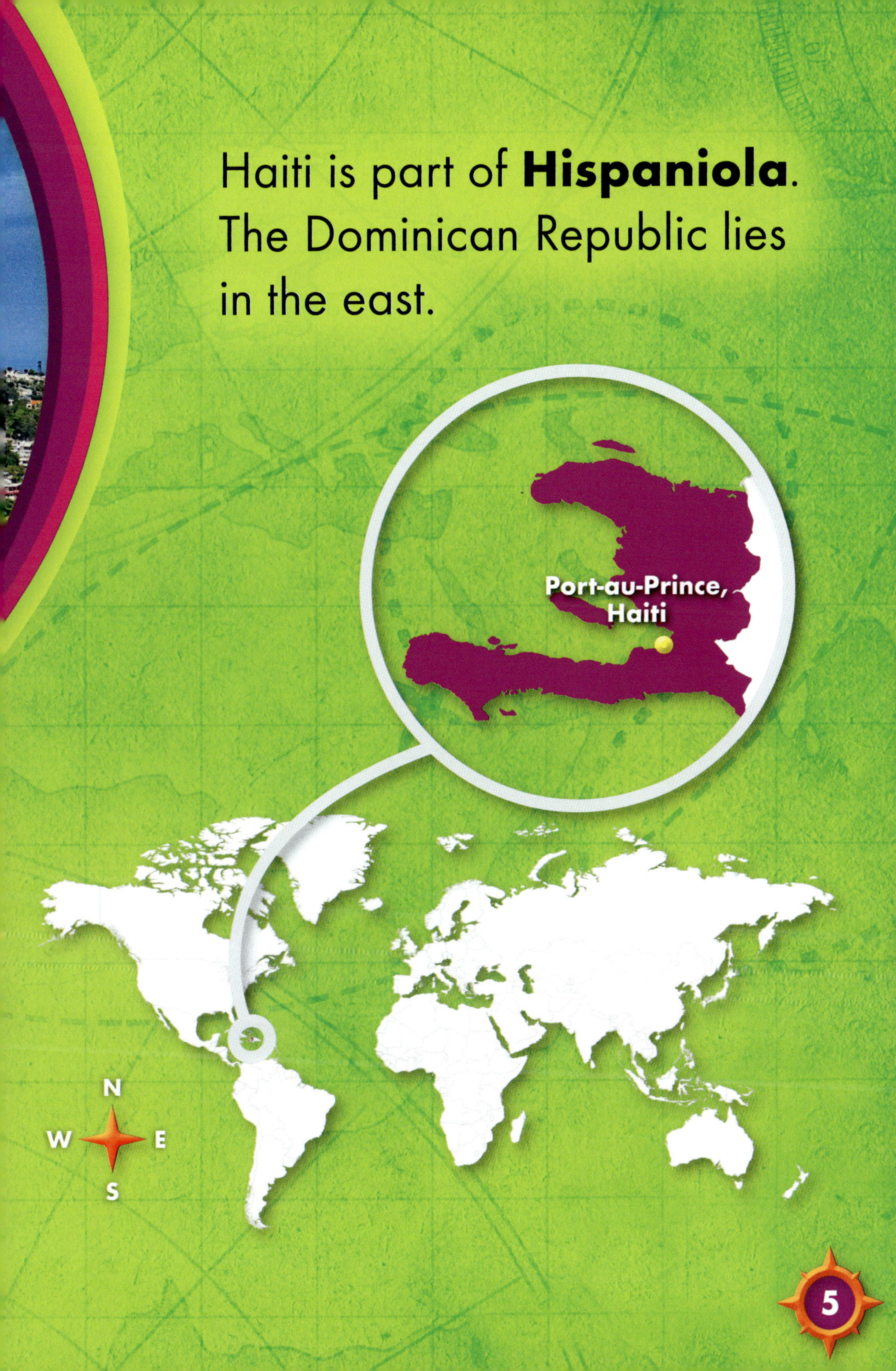

## Land and Animals

Mountains cover most of the country. Cliffs rise on the coasts.

There are two big **peninsulas**. A wide **gulf** separates them.

## Pic la Selle

**Size:** 8,789 feet (2,679 meters) tall

**Famous For:** the tallest mountain in Haiti, part of a group of mountains called the Massif de la Selle

Haiti is **tropical**. The country has two rainy seasons. They are in spring and fall.

**Hurricanes** often hit the southern peninsula.

Lake Azuéi is home to hundreds of crocodiles. Trogons fly in forests.

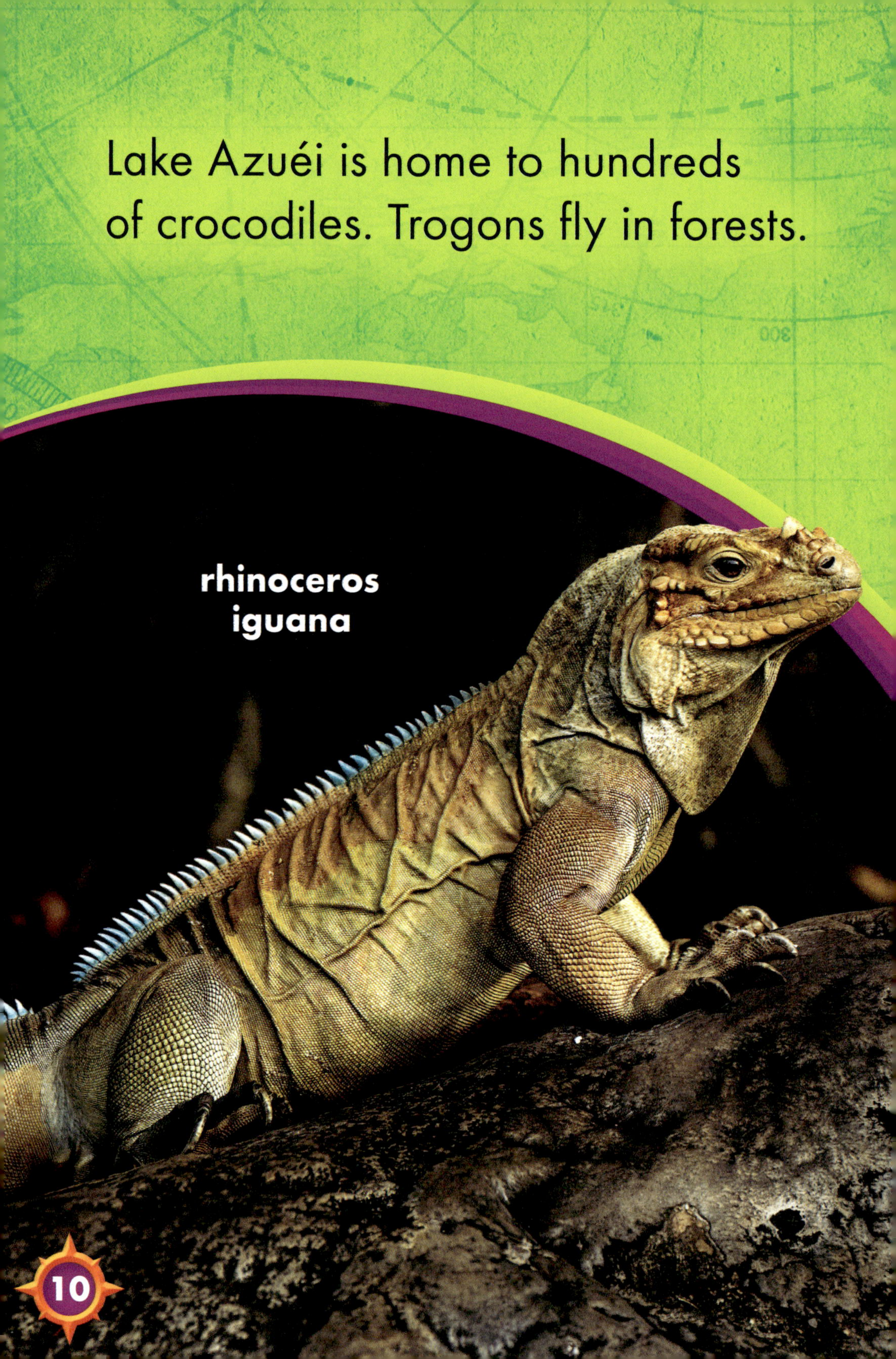

rhinoceros iguana

## Animals of Haiti

American crocodile

Hispaniolan trogon

rhinoceros iguana

Waterhouse's leaf-nosed bat

Iguanas eat leaves and flowers. Bats fly at night. They hunt bugs!

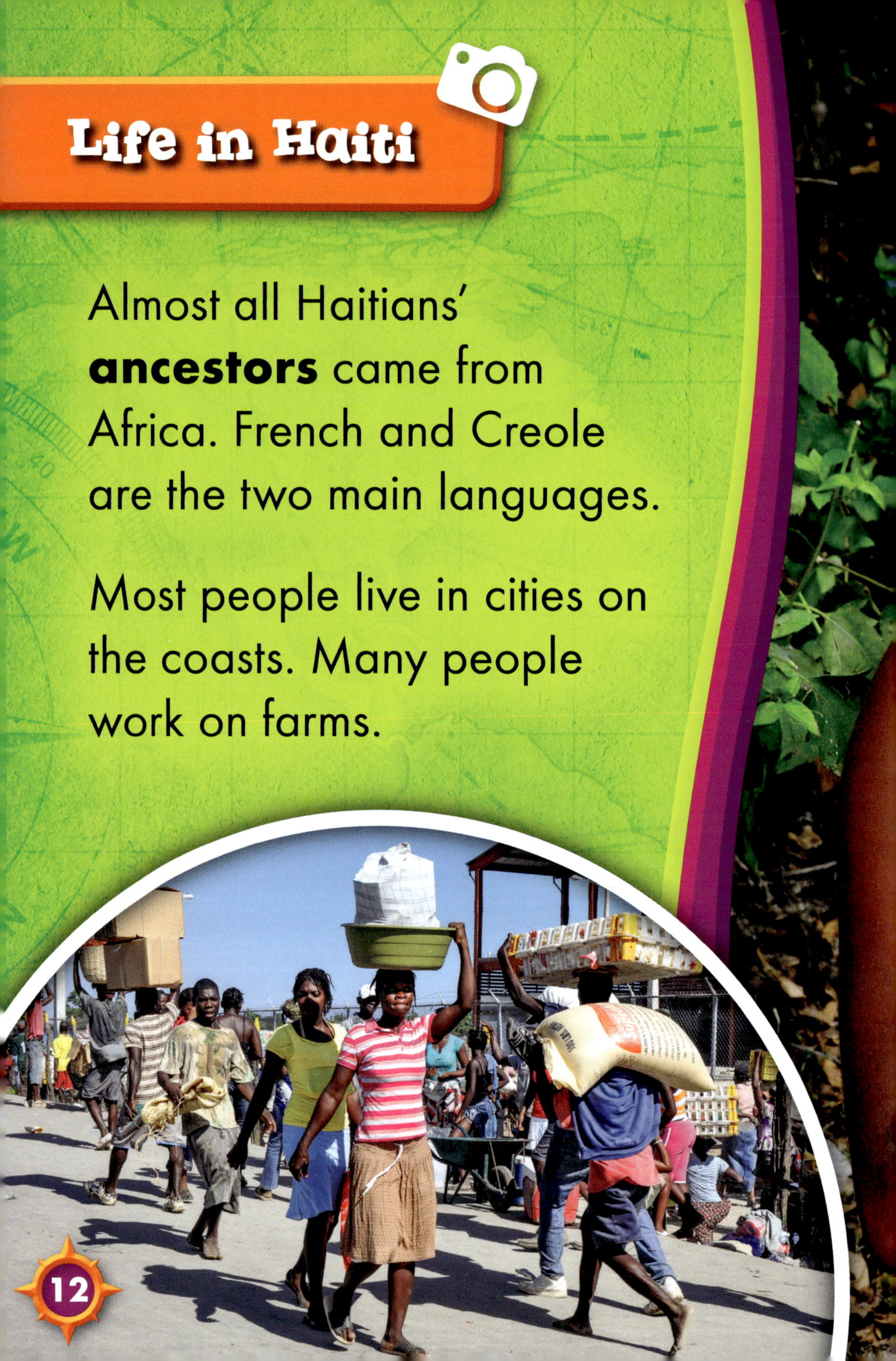

# Life in Haiti

Almost all Haitians' **ancestors** came from Africa. French and Creole are the two main languages.

Most people live in cities on the coasts. Many people work on farms.

English: Hello
French: Bonjour
(bawn-ZHOOR)
Creole: Bonjou
(bawn-ZHOO)

Haiti is home to many artists. People dance and play music called merengue.

Many people play cards or dominoes. Soccer is a popular sport.

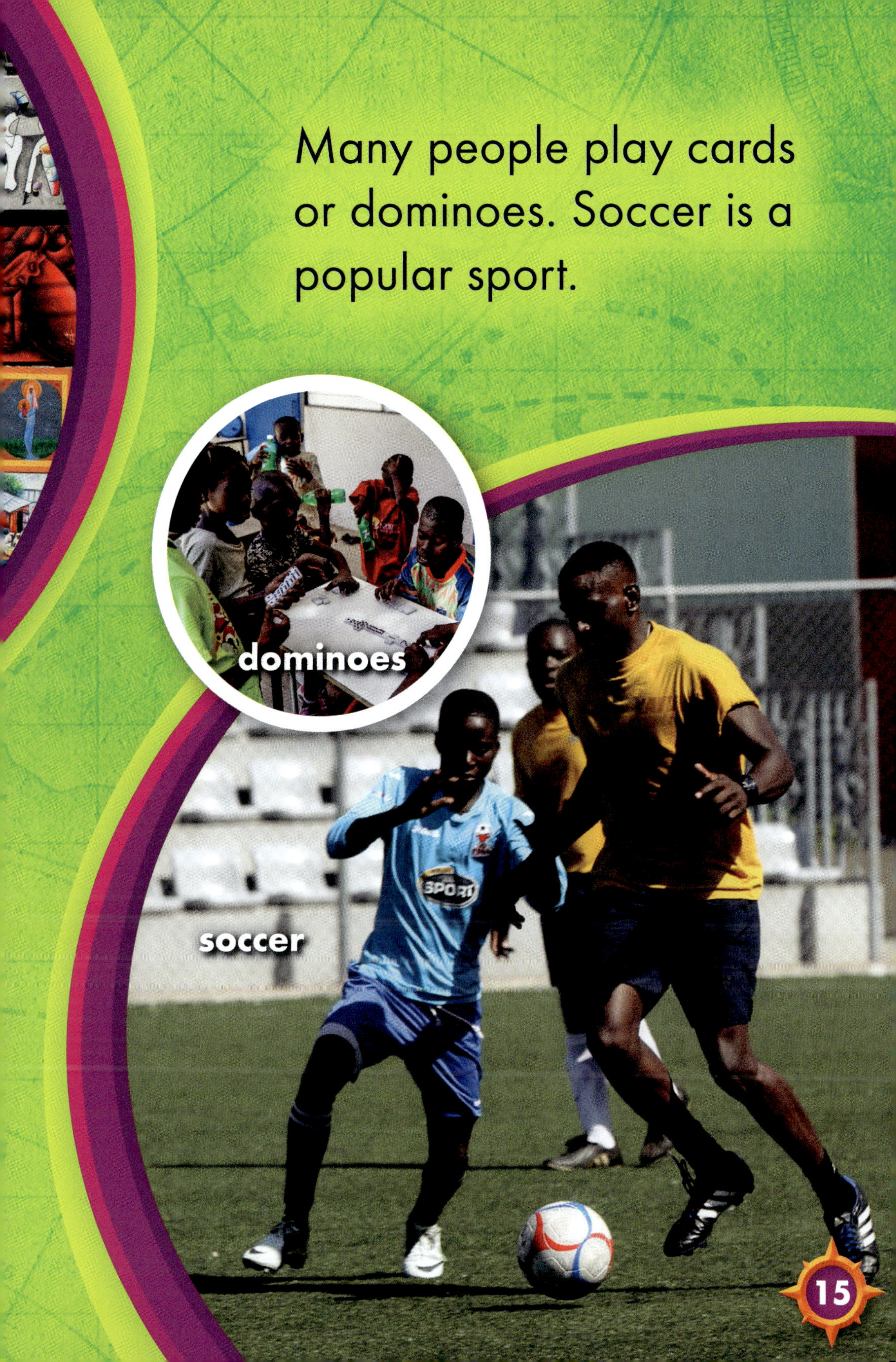

Many Haitians enjoy *griyo*. It is a dish with fried pork. *Pikliz* is pickled vegetables.

Soup *joumou* is made with pumpkin or squash. *Papitas* are a popular snack.

January 1 is Haitian Independence Day. Families enjoy soup *joumou* together.

Carnival

Carnival is a **festival** with music and parades. People dance in colorful costumes. Haitians love their **culture**!

# Haiti Facts

**Size:**
10,714 square miles
(27,750 square kilometers)

**Population:**
11,753,943 (2024)

**National Holiday:**
Independence Day (January 1)

**Main Languages:**
French, Creole

**Capital City:**
Port-au-Prince

## Famous Face

**Name:** Garcelle Beauvais

**Famous For:** an actor in many TV shows and movies, including *Spider-Man: Homecoming*

## Religions

Vodou: 2%

other: 4%

none: 10%

Christian: 84%

## Top Landmarks

Bassin Bleu

*Citadelle Laferrière*

Iron Market

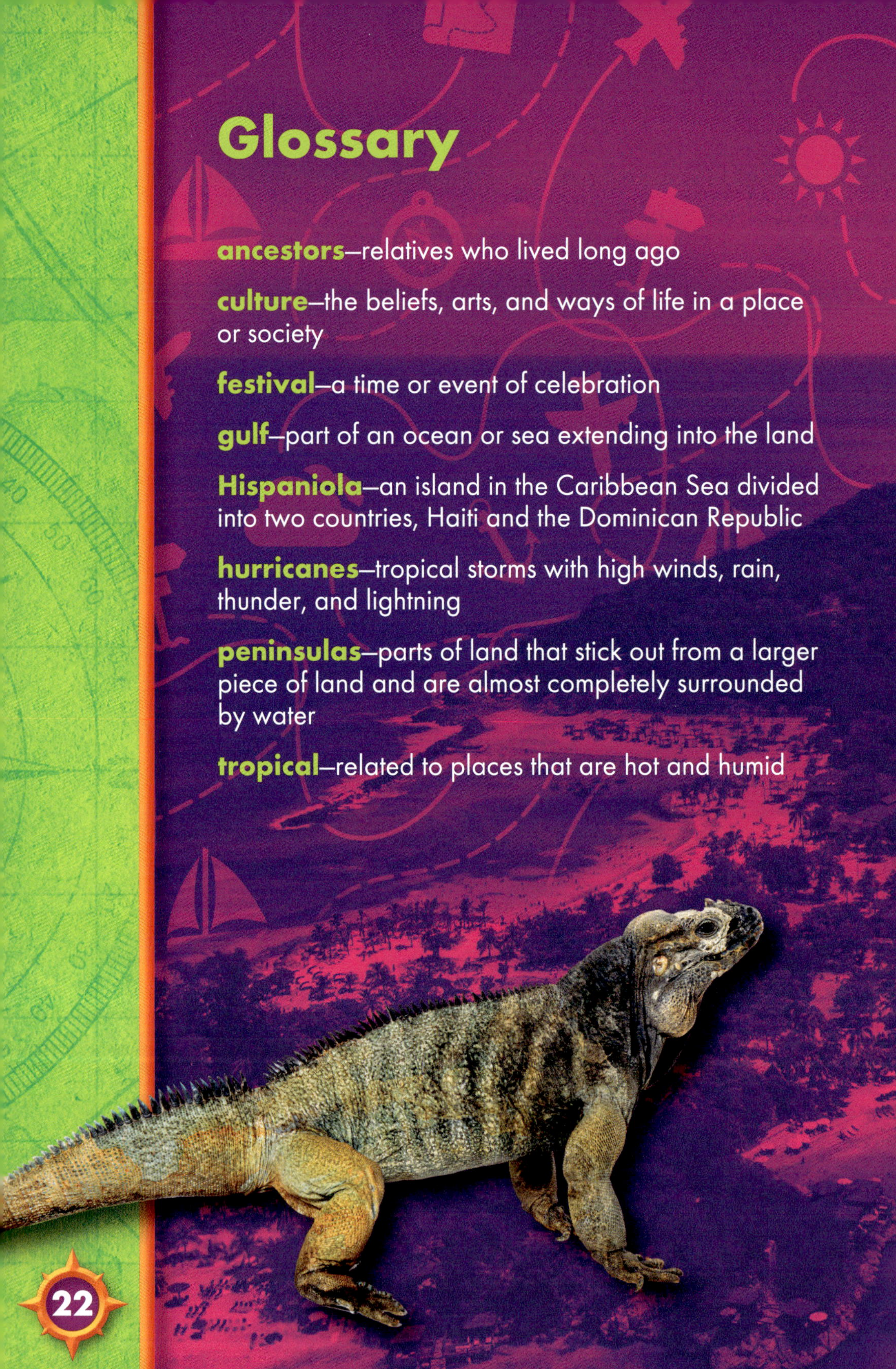

# Glossary

**ancestors**–relatives who lived long ago

**culture**–the beliefs, arts, and ways of life in a place or society

**festival**–a time or event of celebration

**gulf**–part of an ocean or sea extending into the land

**Hispaniola**–an island in the Caribbean Sea divided into two countries, Haiti and the Dominican Republic

**hurricanes**–tropical storms with high winds, rain, thunder, and lightning

**peninsulas**–parts of land that stick out from a larger piece of land and are almost completely surrounded by water

**tropical**–related to places that are hot and humid

# To Learn More

## AT THE LIBRARY

Barnes, Rachael. *The Dominican Republic.* Minneapolis, Minn.: Bellwether Media, 2023.

StJohn, Amanda. *Bouki Cuts Wood: A Haitian Folktale*. Parker, Colo.: The Child's World, 2025.

Williams-Harry, Donette. *Carnival Queen.* Wilton, Conn.: Tiger Tales, 2026.

## ON THE WEB

**FACTSURFER**

Factsurfer.com gives you a safe, fun way to find more information.

1. Go to www.factsurfer.com.
2. Enter "Haiti" into the search box and click 🔍.
3. Select your book cover to see a list of related content.

# Index



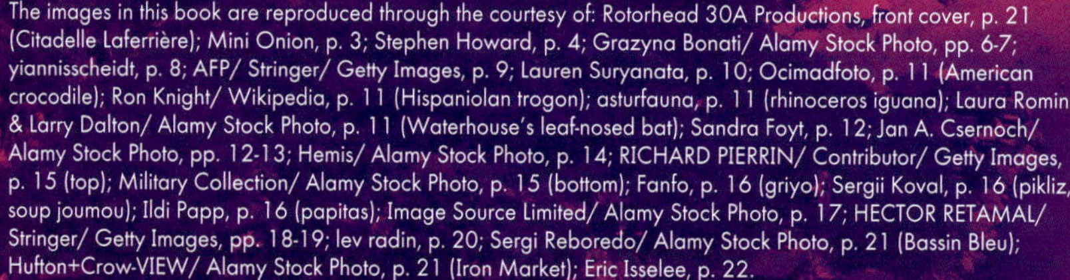

The images in this book are reproduced through the courtesy of: Rotorhead 30A Productions, front cover, p. 21 (Citadelle Laferrière); Mini Onion, p. 3; Stephen Howard, p. 4; Grazyna Bonati/ Alamy Stock Photo, pp. 6-7; yiannisscheidt, p. 8; AFP/ Stringer/ Getty Images, p. 9; Lauren Suryanata, p. 10; Ocimadfoto, p. 11 (American crocodile); Ron Knight/ Wikipedia, p. 11 (Hispaniolan trogon); asturfauna, p. 11 (rhinoceros iguana); Laura Romin & Larry Dalton/ Alamy Stock Photo, p. 11 (Waterhouse's leaf-nosed bat); Sandra Foyt, p. 12; Jan A. Csernoch/ Alamy Stock Photo, pp. 12-13; Hemis/ Alamy Stock Photo, p. 14; RICHARD PIERRIN/ Contributor/ Getty Images, p. 15 (top); Military Collection/ Alamy Stock Photo, p. 15 (bottom); Fanfo, p. 16 (griyo); Sergii Koval, p. 16 (pikliz, soup joumou); Ildi Papp, p. 16 (papitas); Image Source Limited/ Alamy Stock Photo, p. 17; HECTOR RETAMAL/ Stringer/ Getty Images, pp. 18-19; lev radin, p. 20; Sergi Reboredo/ Alamy Stock Photo, p. 21 (Bassin Bleu); Hufton+Crow-VIEW/ Alamy Stock Photo, p. 21 (Iron Market); Eric Isselee, p. 22.